K-5 STEM
Seattle, WA

TAJ MAHAL

Christine Webster

AV² provides enriched content that supplements and complements this book. Weigl's AV² books strive to create inspired learning and engage young minds in a total learning experience.

Your AV² Media Enhanced books come alive with...

Audio
Listen to sections of the book read aloud.

Key Words
Study vocabulary, and complete a matching word activity.

Video
Watch informative video clips.

Quizzes
Test your knowledge.

Go to **www.av2books.com**, and enter this book's unique code.

BOOK CODE

Z976850

Embedded Weblinks
Gain additional information for research.

Slide Show
View images and captions, and prepare a presentation.

AV² by Weigl brings you media enhanced books that support active learning.

Try This!
Complete activities and hands-on experiments.

... and much, much more!

Published by AV² by Weigl
350 5th Avenue, 59th Floor
New York, NY 10118
Website: www.weigl.com   www.av2books.com

Library of Congress Cataloging-in-Publication Data

Webster, Christine
 Taj Mahal / Christine Webster.
   p. cm. -- (Virtual field trips)
 ISBN 978-1-61690-765-5 (hardcover : alk. paper) -- ISBN 978-1-61690-769-3 (paperpack : alk. paper) -- ISBN 978-1-61690-436-4 (online)
 1. Taj Mahal (Agra, India)--Juvenile literature. 2. Agra (India)--Buildings, structures, etc.--Juvenile literature. I. Title.
 NA6183.K57 2011
 726'.809542--dc23
                   2011019315

Printed in the United States of America in North Mankato, Minnesota
2 3 4 5 6 7 8 9 0 17 16 15 14 13

072013
WEP18072013

Editor: Heather Kissock
Design: Terry Paulhus

Every reasonable effort has been made to trace ownership and to obtain permission to reprint copyright material. The publishers would be pleased to have any errors or omissions brought to their attention so that they may be corrected in subsequent printings.

Weigl acknowledges Getty Images as its primary image supplier for this title.

Contents

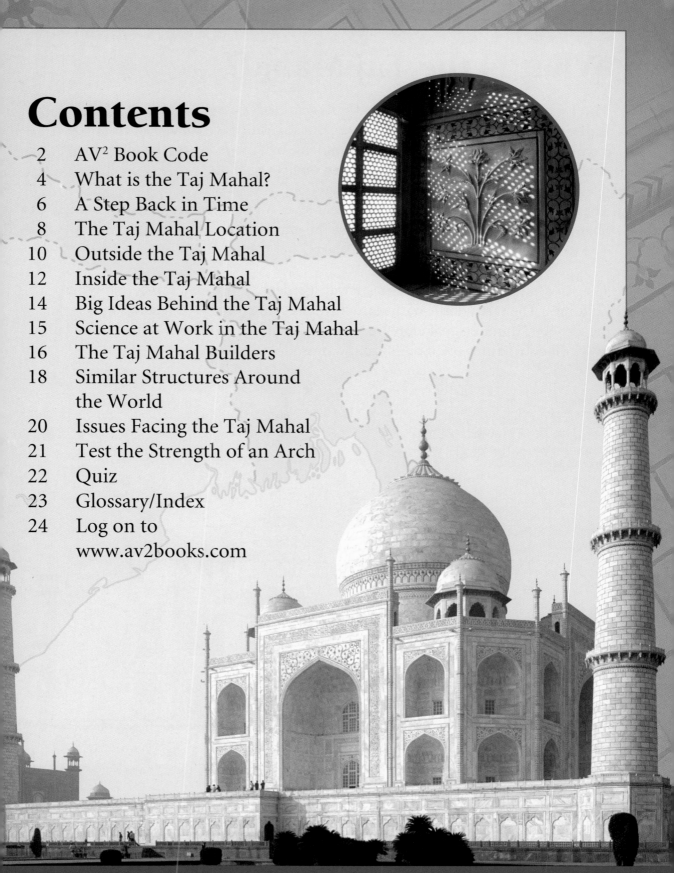

What is the Taj Mahal?

The Taj Mahal is known worldwide for its marbled beauty. Located in Agra, India, on the bank of the Yamuna River, the Taj Mahal is a mausoleum. This is a type of building that is used as a monument. In a mausoleum, the monument encloses the burial site or tomb of a loved one.

The Taj Mahal was built because of a great love. A grief-stricken emperor named Shah Jahan built the Taj Mahal to house the grave of his wife, Mumtaz Mahal. The words Taj Mahal mean "Crown Palace."

The Taj Mahal consists of a main gateway, gardens, a **mosque**, tomb, and other buildings. The main dome of the structure rises more than 200 feet (61 meters) in the air. Four minarets make up the four corners of the structure. Minarets are tall, tower-like structures often built around mosques.

Today, the Taj Mahal is considered to be one of the Seven Wonders of the Modern World. These are structures that are known all over the world for their unique construction.

Snapshot of India

India is located in southern Asia. It is the seventh largest country in the world by size. The country is bordered by water on three sides. The Indian Ocean lies to its south. To its east is the Bay of Bengal. West of India lies the Arabian Sea. India shares its northern borders with Pakistan, Bhutan, China, Nepal, Bangladesh, and Myanmar.

INTRODUCING INDIA

CAPITAL CITY: New Delhi

FLAG:

POPULATION: 1.2 billion (2011)

OFFICIAL LANGUAGES: Hindi, English

CURRENCY: Rupee

CLIMATE: Tropical, dominated by **monsoons**, heat, and humidity

SUMMER TEMPERATURE: Average of 90° Fahrenheit (32° Celsius)

WINTER TEMPERATURE: 50° to 59° Fahrenheit (10° to 15° Celsius)

TIME ZONE: Indian Standard Time (IST)

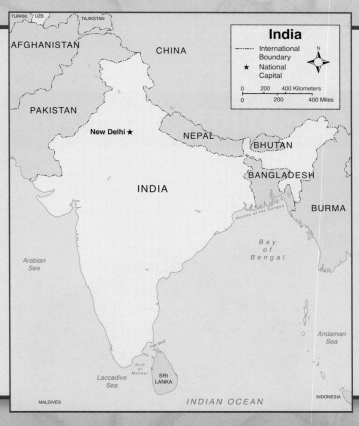

Hindi Words to Know

When visiting a foreign country, it is always a good idea to know some words and phrases of the local language. Practice the phrases below to prepare for a trip to India.

Krip-Ya
Please

Namaskar
Hello

Dhanyavad
Thank you

Kya aap meri madad kar saktey hain?
Can you help me?

Nahi
No

Haa
Yes

Is ke kitnay?
How much is this?

Mera naam … hai
My name is

Maaf kijiye
Sorry

Kya app angrezi aatee hai?
Do you speak English?

Ap kaise hain?
How are you?

Aapka naam kya hai?
What is your name?

A Step Back In Time

India was once controlled by **Muslim** rulers known as the Mughals. Shah Jahan was a Mughal emperor. As emperor, he chose several wives. His favorite wife was named Mumtaz Mahal. Shah Jahan and Mumtaz Mahal had 14 children together. After the birth of their 14th child, however, Mumtaz became ill and died. Shah Jahan was devastated. To honor his wife, he decided to build her the greatest mausoleum on Earth.

CONSTRUCTION TIMELINE

1592
Shah Jahan is born on January 15.

1593
Mumtaz Mahal is born.

1612
Shah Jahan marries Mumtaz Mahal.

1627
Shah Jahan becomes emperor.

1631
Mumtaz Mahal dies following childbirth.

As Shah Jahan's favorite wife, Mumtaz Mahal was one of his closest advisers. She helped him make decisions about his land and its people.

Following Mumtaz Mahal's death, Shah Jahan locked himself in his room for eight days.

Building the Taj Mahal took much planning. Shah Jahan wanted the Taj Mahal to be unique. He wanted to build the entire structure out of white marble. He also planned to decorate it with expensive jewels. Construction of the Taj Mahal complex began in 1632 and took more than 20 years to complete. When it was completed, Shah Jahan often went there to honor his wife.

Shah Jahan ruled the Mughal Empire for 30 years.

1632
Construction of the Taj Mahal, Mumtaz Mahal's tomb, begins.

1643
The mausoleum and some of the surrounding buildings are completed.

1653
The rest of the surrounding buildings and garden are completed.

1666
Shah Jahan dies and is buried next to Mumtaz Mahal.

1861
The Archeological Survey is created to preserve monuments of India and to restore the Taj Mahal and other Agra buildings.

At one time, each of the Taj Mahal's gardens was filled with more than 400 plants.

The Taj Mahal Location

Six months after his wife's death, Shah Jahan laid the **foundation** of the Taj Mahal. To put the concept into place, he first had to choose a site. He chose a 42-acre (17-hectare) area on the bank of the Yamuna River, near his palace in Agra.

The Taj Mahal stands at the far end of the grounds. A four-part garden includes reflecting pools, footpaths, fountains, and trees. Two identical, red sandstone buildings were constructed on the northeastern and northwestern sides of the garden. Facing east is the mosque. The rest house faces west. A red sandstone and marble gate adorns the southern end of the complex.

The Taj Mahal is located 900 feet (274 m) from the main entrance to the complex.

The Taj Mahal Today

More than three million people visit the Taj Mahal each year. In 1983, it was designated a World Heritage Site by the **United Nations Educational, Scientific and Cultural Organization (UNESCO)**. As such, the Taj Mahal is considered a place of cultural heritage that must be preserved for future generations.

Height The building's main dome is 240 feet (73 m) high. The main structure is 186 feet (57 m) high on each side. Each corner of the structure has a minaret that is 131 feet (40 m) high.

Area The Taj Mahal is set on a square platform. Its four minarets are set on an octagonal base. The garden is rectangular in shape. It is 1,050 feet by 984 feet (320 m x 300 m).

240 Feet

131 Feet

186 Feet

984 Feet

1,050 Feet

Outside the Taj Mahal

The Taj Mahal is best known for its exterior. Its graceful domes, tall minarets, and pristine, white marble are known throughout the world. The gardens, pools, and footpaths leading up to the building only add to its peaceful splendor.

Dome The Taj Mahal is easily recognized by its large dome. The dome sits above the center of the building and has four smaller domes around it. The large dome has a false ceiling inside, which makes the dome smaller on the inside. The top of the dome is decorated with a lotus flower pattern, which represents good fortune, and a **finial**. A jewelled inlay circles around the dome's drum.

The shape of the main dome is often compared to an onion.

Like the main dome, each minaret is capped with a lotus flower design and finial.

Minarets Minarets are an important part of Muslim architecture. They are where the call to prayer originates. Each of the Taj Mahal's four minarets has three balconies. They are connected by a winding stairway. The minarets were built with an outward slant. This was done so that, if they ever came down, they would fall away from the main building.

The exterior walls of the plinth feature carvings of leaves and other plants.

Plinth The Taj Mahal stands on a raised platform, called a plinth, that is 22 feet (6.7 m) high. It covers 1,023 square feet (95 square meters). The plinth looks pure white from a distance, but its marble is actually decorated with jewels and elaborate designs. A double staircase on the plinth provides access to the tomb itself.

Symmetry When viewing the Taj Mahal, it appears to be in perfect balance. Whatever is on one side of the building is found in the same position on the other side. All of the **arches**, minarets, and domes have been positioned this way. This balance is called symmetry. It adds to the illusion of perfection at the site.

The Taj Mahal retains its symmetry from every angle.

Decoration Much of the Taj Mahal's marble is decorated with either jewels or **calligraphy**, which have been inlaid or carved into the stone. Flowers and geometric shapes are the most common patterns used. Calligraphy often refers to the Qu'ran, the religious scriptures of the Muslim people.

To make the carvings, artists would draw the flower patterns directly on the marble. They would then use chisels to carve them out.

Iwan Each side of the Taj Mahal features a large, arched iwan, or porch. Beside each iwan are two levels of similar, but smaller, iwans. Another set of small iwans sits on an angle next to them. These smaller iwans help make the Taj Mahal look larger than it actually is.

The large iwans are decorated with gems and colored stones.

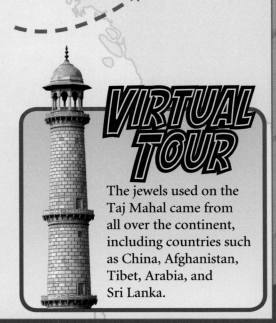
VIRTUAL TOUR

The jewels used on the Taj Mahal came from all over the continent, including countries such as China, Afghanistan, Tibet, Arabia, and Sri Lanka.

Inside the Taj Mahal

The interior of the Taj Mahal matches, and in some places exceeds, the splendor of the building's outside.

Central Chamber The central chamber is located underneath the main dome. The high roof gives it an open appearance. The room is in the shape of an octagon. Each side of the octagon serves as an entrance to the room. In the middle of the chamber are two **cenotaphs**, representing the graves of Shah Jahan and Mumtaz Mahal. They are not in the cenotaphs, however. Their actual graves are found in the **crypt** directly below the room.

The central chamber is surrounded by two floors of archways. Some archways provide outside light. Others lead to connecting rooms

A marble screen surrounds the cenotaphs. The screen is decorated with gemstones placed in floral patterns.

Cenotaphs The cenotaphs for Shah Jahan and Mumtaz Mahal lie beside each other. Mumtaz Mahal's cenotaph is located directly under the center of the dome. The cenotaph for Shah Jahan is to the left. His memorial sits slightly higher than hers. A lamp hangs above the cenotaphs. The light from this lamp is meant to burn forever. Both cenotaphs are decorated with jewels and calligraphy. The calligraphy identifies each of them and quotes the Qu'ran.

Crypt The crypt is where both Shah Jahan and Mumtaz Mahal are buried. Muslims do not believe that elaborate decoration is appropriate for burial sites, so the room itself is quite plain. ▪ ▪ ▪ ➤

The crypt is not open to the public. People must have special permission to enter it.

Each level of the interior has four corner rooms and a room on each side.

Connecting Chambers Each of the Taj Mahal's two floors has eight separate rooms branching off from the central chamber. It has been suggested that they were built to house the tombs of other members of the royal family. However, many people believe that they were used for prayers and music.

Hallways The rooms on each floor are linked by a system of hallways. Screens made from marble extend along the walls. Like most of the Taj Mahal, the screens have floral and geometric shapes carved into them.

The marble screens in the Taj Mahal are called jali screens.

Big Ideas Behind the Taj Mahal

A monument such as the Taj Mahal needed the strongest materials. It also needed to be designed in a way that would allow the building to stand for a long time. Shah Jahan designed the Taj Mahal using ancient scientific principles that are still used.

India has a vast supply of marble. The Taj Mahal's marble came from a nearby town called Makrana. The marble used is called Makrana marble.

The Properties of Marble

Shah Jahan chose marble because of its availability, its texture, and its beauty. Marble is known as a soft rock. This means that it can be easily cut and shaped. The measurement of hardness scale (MOHS) determines the hardness of a stone based on how easily it can be scratched by grit or hard objects. On this scale, marble is a three out of ten. A hard piece of plastic rates about 2 on this scale. It could not scratch marble. However, quartz, which measures 7, will scratch marble. Marble's softness allows the rock to be sculpted into beautiful artistic shapes by creating grooves and straight edges. It is often used for sculpting and building.

Arches

Arches have been used to support structures since 300 BC. Above its foundation, the Taj Mahal is supported by arched **vaults**. By building an archway, heavy weights can be supported. The weight of a structure presses downward. With an arch, this is changed from a downward force to an outward force. The outward force spreads the weight of the structure evenly across a larger area. Ancient arches are built from stone. Today, they can be constructed from wood, concrete, wire, and brick.

The pointed arches are a main feature of the Taj Mahal. They are found throughout the building.

Science at Work in the Taj Mahal

Building the Taj Mahal was a long and difficult process. The workers did not have the technology found in the world today. People had to use the technology that was available to them at the time.

Marble forms the face of the Taj Mahal, but underneath the marble is a base of bricks. The two materials are bonded together with mortar and iron clamps.

Strength in Form

The Taj Mahal was built stone by stone. Marble blocks had to be laid in such a way that would give the building the greatest strength as a whole. To create this strength, the blocks were layered on top of each other in a pattern. Each rectangular block of marble was about 15 to 18 inches (38 to 46 centimeters) thick. One block was placed lengthwise. Another was placed beside the first with its short end facing outward. The pattern repeated on each row and layer. Each block was **fused** with a mixture of **mortar**. Iron clamps held the blocks in place. This system of long and short blocks helped support the heavy walls. It also stopped blocks from coming loose later on.

Simple Machines

Workers relied on simple machines to help them with the construction of the Taj Mahal. Ramps were used to lift heavy slabs of marble. A ramp is a type of simple machine called an inclined plane. A plane is a flat surface. When it is slanted, or inclined, at an angle other than a right angle, it can help move objects across distances. To help lift heavy items, workers used pulleys and ropes. A pulley is made up of a wheel with a groove along the edge. This groove holds a rope in place. One end of the rope is attached to the load being moved. The other end is pulled by a human or an animal. The pulley eases the weight of the load so that the object is easier to lift.

Mules and oxen were used to pull the ropes that operated the pulleys.

VIRTUAL TOUR

More than 1,000 elephants were used to transport materials to the Taj Mahal site.

The Taj Mahal Builders

It is not known who actually designed the Taj Mahal. Architects from around the world were called upon to help create the structure. However, a man named Ustad Isa is most often noted as the main designer of the Taj Mahal. He was assisted by several **artisans**, who helped make the Taj Mahal beautiful.

The Red Fort is also called the Delhi Fort. Made of red sandstone, its walls are 1.5 miles (2.5 kilometers) long and have heights of 60 feet (18 meters) to 110 feet (34 m).

Ustad Isa Chief Designer

Ustad Isa was an architect, mathematician, and astronomer. Some historians believe that Ustad was the architect of the Red Fort, Shah Jahan's palace. This is one of the reasons he is often given credit for designing the Taj Mahal as well. Other people believe that an Italian named Geronimo Veroneo designed the Taj Mahal. In 1640, a monk visited Agra and met Veroneo. He wrote that Veroneo was responsible for the design. There is little evidence to support this claim, however. Other people who may have designed the Taj Mahal include Ustad Ahmad Lahori and Isa Muhammad Effendi.

Ismail Khan Dome Designer

Ismail Khan designed the main dome of the Taj Mahal. He was from the **Ottoman Empire** and was considered one of the best designers of domes in that era.

The construction of the main dome is believed to have taken 12 years.

Amanat Khan Chief Calligrapher

Amanat Khan, from Persia, was the Taj Mahal's main calligrapher. His name is inscribed on the gateway to the Taj Mahal.

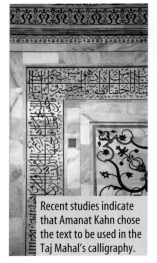

Recent studies indicate that Amanat Kahn chose the text to be used in the Taj Mahal's calligraphy.

Amir Ali Master Stonecutter

Amir Ali, from the Baluchistan part of Iran, was the Taj Mahal's master stonecutter. He gave his expertise in designing the marble blocks that make up the foundation and walls of the Taj Mahal.

Amir Ali supervised a team of stonecutters to ensure that the work was done properly.

Masons

Masons are people who work with stones or bricks. Building the Taj Mahal required the skills of many masons. When the raw marble slabs arrived at the construction site, each slab had to be shaped and smoothed. Masons used an L-shaped tool called a square to measure the pieces to size. The masons scratched the measurements onto the marble. Then, with a chisel and mallet, they would strike the marble. Once the stone was roughly the right shape, a smaller tool was used to remove tiny edges. The stone was then shaped into a flat, rectangular block and was polished. The mason slid an iron plate with coarse or fine sand across the stone. This acted as sandpaper, making the marble smooth as glass.

Sometimes, a mason would carve a symbol, or mason's mark, into the marble. This showed others who designed this "piece of art."

Calligraphers

Today, calligraphy is still considered to be an art form.

Calligraphers specialize in the art of fine handwriting. Calligraphy may be used to decorate buildings or art pieces. There are many different forms of calligraphy, depending on the part of the world, language, or culture that is being presented by the calligrapher. On the Taj Mahal, calligraphers used scrolls to inscribe passages into the gate and the walls around the Taj Mahal.

Laborers

Laborers were responsible for bringing the marble to the Taj Mahal site. They led teams of oxen over ramps and hauled water from the river. The water was mixed to make mortar to hold the bricks together. Laborers built scaffolding so that there were platforms to build the brick walls higher. They also shimmied over the dome area to lay the bricks.

Scaffolding is like a ladder. It has platforms at each level and is easy to climb.

Similar Structures Around the World

Throughout history, people have used stone to build many structures. The ancient Egyptians used stone to construct the Great Pyramids. In Greece, architects designed structures such as the Parthenon from marble. Like the Taj Mahal, these structures are well known around the world. However, there are many other important stone buildings that were constructed in India during the Mughal rule.

Bibi Ka Maqbara

BUILT: 1678
LOCATION: Aurangabad, Maharashtra
DESIGN: Prince Azam Shah
DESCRIPTION: Shah Jahan's son, Aurangzeb, built this temple to rival the Taj Mahal. Like his father, Aurangzeb built this mausoleum for his wife—Rabia-ud-Durrani. Aurangzeb's son, Azam Shah, was the designer. It was built at the end of the Mughal reign. It is smaller than the Taj Mahal and cost less to build.

Bibi Ka Maqbara translates to "Tomb of the Lady." It is often referred to as the Poor Man's Taj Mahal due to its inferior materials and size.

Itmad-Ud-Daulah's Tomb

Some people believe that Itmad-Ud-Daulah's Tomb was the inspiration for the Taj Mahal's design.

BUILT: 1622–1628
LOCATION: Agra, Uttar Pradesh
DESIGN: Nur Jahan
DESCRIPTION: Itmad-Ud-Daulah's Tomb is located on the left side of the Yamuna River. This mausoleum is nicknamed the Baby Taj. Nur Jahan built the tomb for her father, Mirza Ghiyas Beg. As a government official, he was given the name Itmad-Ud-Daulah. He was Mumtaz Mahal's grandfather.

Jama Masjid

BUILT: 1658
LOCATION: Delhi, India
DESIGN: Shah Jahan
DESCRIPTION: The Jama Masjid is a temple, or place of worship, for the people of India. It is the largest mosque in India. It consists of gateways, towers, and two minarets. Each minaret is 131 feet (40 m) high. Visitors may reach the top of the minarets. Here, they can see all of Delhi.

The mosque was built in six years. More than 5,000 people worked on its construction.

Fatehpur Sikri

BUILT: 1571
LOCATION: Uttar Pradesh, India
DESIGN: Mughal Emperor Akbar
DESCRIPTION: This World Heritage Site was built in honor of a saint named Salim Chishti. When the Mughals ruled, it was the political capital. Fatehpur Sikri consists of palaces, halls, and mosques. Panch Mahal is located here. This five-story building has 176 carved columns on its bottom floor.

The pillars of Panch Mahal once had jali screens between them.

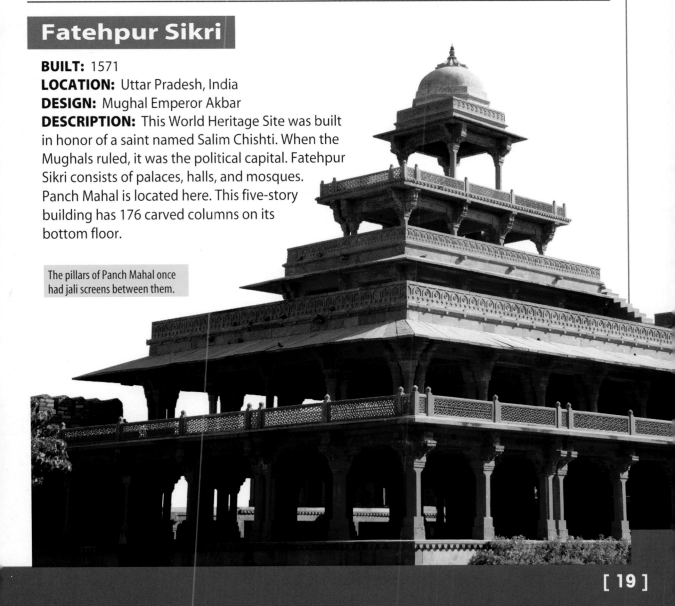

Issues Facing the Taj Mahal

The city of Agra was built on the western bank of the Yamuna River in 1475. When the Mughal rulers took over the city, it flourished. Forts, buildings, and tombs were built during this time. Today, millions of people visit India each year. This has taken a toll on the Taj Mahal.

WHAT IS THE ISSUE?

The humidity and monsoon rains are damaging the Taj Mahal.

Breathing is creating problems for the Taj Mahal. Every breath a tourist takes sends moisture into the air.

The area is greatly affected by pollution. The city of Agra is **congested**. Thousands of people make their home here and work in the city. The city is crammed with vehicles, people, and factories.

EFFECTS

Water is leaking into the building and **eroding** the marble.

The moisture helps mold grow on the marble. This causes erosion and makes the marble crack.

Thick black smoke from cars and factories sends pollution into the air. As it mixes with moisture, it falls as **acid rain**. The acid rain **corrodes** the Taj Mahal's marble.

ACTION TAKEN

Sealants are being applied to the building to stop water from getting into the Taj Mahal.

The Indian government has increased the price of admission to the site to lower tourist numbers. Restoration programs are also in place to repair the marble.

The government of India has banned vehicles that use gas from the area. It has also closed down many factories that send chemicals into the air. Attempts are also being made to clean the Yamuna River.

Test the Strength of an Arch

Arches are used to support heavy weights. They use minimal materials. They are cost-efficient and strong. Arches are also architecturally attractive. Try this activity to see how arches really work.

Materials
- Six eggs
- Heavy books
- Cellophane tape
- Scissors

Instructions

1. Break off the smallest end of each egg. Pour the insides into a bowl. Store them in fridge to cook or bake with later. Throw out the broken ends.

2. Take six long pieces of cellophane tape. Wind them around the center of each eggshell.

3. Cut through the center of the tape. You should now have six dome-shaped shells.

4. Lay the six domes on a table in a rectangle. Make sure the flat side is down.

5. Estimate how many books you can lay across the domes.

6. Now, lay books one by one across the domes. See how many books you can lay down before the shells break.

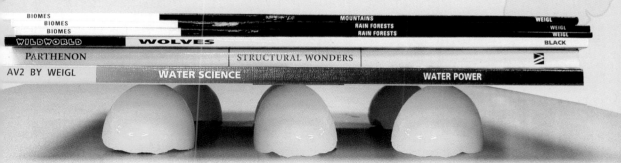

Taj Mahal Quiz

Q Why was marble chosen to build the Taj Mahal?

A Marble was chosen for its availability, its texture, and its beauty.

Q Why were arches used?

A Arches support extreme weights evenly by changing the downward force of the building to an outward force.

Q Why were the marble slabs placed lengthwise and then widthwise?

A This gave the structure strength. It also prevented the bricks from coming loose.

Q Name two simple machines that were used to build the Taj Mahal.

A Ramps and pulleys.

Glossary

acid rain: air pollution produced when acid chemicals are incorporated into rain, snow, fog, or mist

arches: curved structures that span an opening

artisans: craftspeople

calligraphy: a highly decorative type of handwriting

cenotaphs: monuments honoring a person or persons whose remains are elsewhere

congested: overcrowded or thick

corrodes: eats away

crypt: an underground chamber used as a burial site

eroding: wearing away

finial: a sculptured ornament that sits at the top of a structure

foundation: the base on which something stands

fused: united by melting

masons: people skilled in building with stone

monsoons: winds that change direction with the seasons, blowing in steadily from one direction for as long as six months and then blowing from the opposite direction for the other six

mortar: a mixture of lime, sand, and water, used as a bond between bricks

mosque: a Muslim place of worship

Muslim: a follower of the Islamic religion

Ottoman Empire: a former Turkish empire in Europe, Asia, and Africa, which lasted from the late 13th century until the end of World War I

sealants: substances used to seal a surface to prevent passage of a liquid or gas

United Nations Educational, Scientific, and Cultural Organization (UNESCO): an agency that encourages international peace and universal respect by promoting collaboration among nations

vaults: arched structures that form a roof or ceiling

Index

Log on to www.av2books.com

AV² by Weigl brings you media enhanced books that support active learning. Go to www.av2books.com, and enter the special code found on page 2 of this book. You will gain access to enriched and enhanced content that supplements and complements this book. Content includes video, audio, web links, quizzes, a slide show, and activities.

Audio
Listen to sections of the book read aloud.

Video
Watch informative video clips.

Embedded Weblinks
Gain additional information for research.

Try This!
Complete activities and hands-on experiments.

WHAT'S ONLINE?

Try This!	Embedded Weblinks	Video	EXTRA FEATURES
Test your knowledge of Hindi.	Find out more about where the Taj Mahal is located.	Watch a video introduction to the Taj Mahal.	**Audio** Listen to sections of the book read aloud.
Test your knowledge of the history of the Taj Mahal in a timeline activity.	Learn more about a notable person from the history of the Taj Mahal.	Watch a video about another tour destination near the Taj Mahal.	**Key Words** Study vocabulary, and complete a matching word activity.
Learn more about the math behind the Taj Mahal.	Learn more about becoming an architect.		**Slide Show** View images and captions, and prepare a presentation
Compare modern architects with ancient ones.	Find out more about other important structures near the Taj Mahal.		**Quizzes** Test your knowledge.
Write about an issue in your community that is similar to one facing the Taj Mahal.			
Complete a fun, interactive activity about the Taj Mahal.			

AV² was built to bridge the gap between print and digital. We encourage you to tell us what you like and what you want to see in the future.
Sign up to be an AV² Ambassador at www.av2books.com/ambassador.